797,885 Books
are available to read at

Forgotten Books

www.ForgottenBooks.com

Forgotten Books' App
Available for mobile, tablet & eReader

ISBN 978-1-331-27763-7
PIBN 10168045

This book is a reproduction of an important historical work. Forgotten Books uses state-of-the-art technology to digitally reconstruct the work, preserving the original format whilst repairing imperfections present in the aged copy. In rare cases, an imperfection in the original, such as a blemish or missing page, may be replicated in our edition. We do, however, repair the vast majority of imperfections successfully; any imperfections that remain are intentionally left to preserve the state of such historical works.

Forgotten Books is a registered trademark of FB &c Ltd.
Copyright © 2017 FB &c Ltd.
FB &c Ltd, Dalton House, 60 Windsor Avenue, London, SW19 2RR.
Company number 08720141. Registered in England and Wales.

For support please visit www.forgottenbooks.com

1 MONTH OF FREE READING

at

www.ForgottenBooks.com

By purchasing this book you are eligible for one month membership to ForgottenBooks.com, giving you unlimited access to our entire collection of over 700,000 titles via our web site and mobile apps.

To claim your free month visit:

www.forgottenbooks.com/free168045

* Offer is valid for 45 days from date of purchase. Terms and conditions apply.

English
Français
Deutsche
Italiano
Español
Português

www.forgottenbooks.com

Mythology Photography **Fiction** Fishing Christianity **Art** Cooking Essays Buddhism Freemasonry Medicine **Biology** Music **Ancient Egypt** Evolution Carpentry Physics Dance Geology **Mathematics** Fitness Shakespeare **Folklore** Yoga Marketing **Confidence** Immortality Biographies Poetry **Psychology** Witchcraft Electronics Chemistry History **Law** Accounting **Philosophy** Anthropology Alchemy Drama Quantum Mechanics Atheism Sexual Health **Ancient History Entrepreneurship** Languages Sport Paleontology Needlework Islam **Metaphysics** Investment Archaeology Parenting Statistics Criminology **Motivational**

This book is DUE on the last date stamped below

OCT 11 1927

HANDBOOK

OF THE

MINNESOTA

CHILD STUDY ASSOCIATION,

CONTAINING

Suggestions for the Study of Children.

PREPARED BY

E. A. KIRKPATRICK,
S. H. ROWE.
ISABEL LAWRENCE,
A. W. RANKIN,
LILLIAN BLAISDELL.

PRINTED BY THE ASSOCIATION FOR THE USE OF MEMBERS.

PRICE TO THOSE NOT MEMBERS, THIRTY CENTS.

WINONA, MINN.:
JONES & KROEGER, PRINTERS,
1897.

HISTORY OF THE ASSOCIATION.

The way was paved for the organization of this association by letters sent to the educators of the state by Prof. M. V. O'Shea. The first step toward organization was taken at the Summer School Congresses held at the University in August, 1895, when a committee consisting of Prof. L. H. Galbreath, Supt. S. S. Parr and Miss Marietta L. Pierce was appointed to prepare a constitution. The organization was effected at the holiday meeting of the State Educational Association by the adoption of the constitution reported by the committee and by the election of officers. About 80 persons joined at this meeting and as many more during the year 1896. A very few have withdrawn from the Association and a number have joined this year (1897).

The first Secretary-Treasurer of the Association, L. H. Galbreath, before he left the State, in June, 1896, sent out eight communications to members treating of the following topics: Communication I., Child Study Literature; II., Eyes of School Children and Their Defects; III., The Use of Stories and The Child a Volume to be Read; IV., Plan and Method in the Study of Children and Thurber's Outlines for the Study of Children's Reading; V., Rythmic Sense, Movement and other Unnoticed Educative Influences; VI., A Plan for the Study of Memory; VII., A Study of Unexpected and Incorrect Answers of Children; VIII., A Study of Unexpected and Irrelevant Questions of Children. Besides the communications, there were sent to the members pamphlets published by the Iowa and the Michigan departments of public instruction and a special child study number of School Education.

The communications sent out by the present secretary are as follows: IX., General Remarks to Members, The Dull Child the Wise Man's Problem, Children's Habits, A Study of Children's Experiences with Money, Sound Blindness, Adolescence, Mental Images and Test of Accuracy of Incidental Attention and Memory; X., Child Study Literature; XI., Outline for reporting Attempted Improvement of a School and a Pupil. This handbook and a special child study number of School Education will also be sent to all members who have paid their dues this year.

The supply of all the above communications, except a few copies of VI., VII., VIII., X. and XI., is exhausted, but the most valuable parts of some of them are reprinted in this pamphlet.

The meetings of the Association have been a round table and business meeting at the time of organization, a child study day at the Educational meetings at the University Summer School, in 1896, and a round table and Annual meeting at the time of the Minnesota Educational Association, in the holidays. Other meetings will be held this year, in August, at the University and at St. Paul when the State Educational Association meets.

The importance of the subject of child study to teachers has been recognized by the Department of Public Instruction by the employment of three persons to present the matter to the students in the various Summer Schools of the state. The persons appointed for this service were S. S. Parr, President of our association; E. A. Kirkpatrick, Secretary; and J. A. Vandyke, one of the corresponding secretaries.

At the last business meeting a committee of five, consisting of E. A. Kirkpatrick, S. H. Rowe, Isabel Lawrence A. W. Rankin, and Lillian Blaisdell, was appointed to prepare plans for child study, and this pamphlet is the result of their efforts in that direction. It is intended to be what its name implies, a "hand book" for continuous reference and use by all members and of permanent value to all persons doing anything in the line of child study.

The secretary of the association will be glad to correspond with members as to work in child study, receive reports and aid in special investigations in every possible way.

CONSTITUTION OF THE MINNESOTA CHILD STUDY ASSOCIATION.

ARTICLE I.

NAME—The name of this organization shall be the Minnesota Child Study Association.

ARTICLE II.

PURPOSE—The purpose of this Association shall be the promotion of child study.

ARTICLE III.

OFFICERS—The officers of this Association shall be a president, elected for a term of two years, a secretary-treasurer elected for two years, and three directors elected at first for terms of one, two and three years respectively and thereafter, unless for vacancies by death, or resignation, one each year for a term of three years. The officers above named shall constitute the executive board and shall have control of all general business of the Association under forms and limitations customary in such bodies. In all elections voting shall be confined to those who have paid their current membership fees.

ARTICLE IV.

MEMBERSHIP—Any person actively engaged in educational work, or any other person who will sign the membership roll as a pledge to cooperate by active participation in the work of the Association, may, by prepayment of fifty cents into the treasury of the Association, become a member of the same.

ARTICLE V.

MEETINGS—The meetings of this Association shall be of two kinds: general meetings representing all members and centers, and particular meetings of local centers. Each kind of meeting shall occur at such times and places as the body to which it belongs shall determine. All elections shall be by open nominations and written ballot. All orders shall be subject to the usual parliamentary restrictions.

BY-LAWS.

1. All membership fees shall go into the general treasury, provided that no such receipts go to expenses of officers or other outlay of a particular nature unless ordered at the annual meeting.

2. The local organizations shall be by means of centers or round tables which shall organize, hold at least three meetings per year, pay fifty cents per member into the general treasury each year, follow the directions of the parent society and contribute observations and reports properly when called upon.

3. The Association shall make at least one general printed report each year after the first year and one within this year if desirable.

4. This Association shall seek to become a department of the Minnesota State Educational Association.

5. The executive board shall be empowered to appoint a first, second and third vice-president to serve each for one year and whose duty it shall be to organize and manage local centers.

6. Amendments to this constitutions and to these by-laws may be adopted at any regular meeting of the Association provided that such amendments be reported to the executive committee at least twenty-four hours before they are acted upon by the Association.

OFFICERS.

President—S. S. Parr, St. Cloud.

Vice Presidents—First, Charles F. Koehler, Mankato; Second, Henry S. Baker, St. Paul; Third, Harlow Gale, Minneapolis.

Secretary-Treasurer—E. A. Kirkpatrick, Winona.

Advisory Board—Dr. W. A. Mayo and Dr. Charles Mayo, Rochester; Dr. John H. James, Mankato; Dr. J. C. Boehm, St. Cloud; Dr. Chas. N. Hewitt, Red Wing; George A. Merrill, State School, Owatonna; Inspector Geo. B. Aiton, Minneapolis; Supt. W. W. Pendergast, St. Paul.

Corresponding Secretaries—A. E. Engstrom, Cannon Falls; L. C. Lord, Moorhead; K. W. Buell, Spring Valley; George R. Kleeberger, St. Cloud; F. V. Hubbard, Red Wing; Edgar George, St. Peter; E. E. McIntire, Glencoe; J. A. Vandyke, Wabasha; Miss Sarah C. Brooks, St. Paul; Mrs. C. L. Place, St. Paul; Mrs. Alice M. Cooley, Minneapolis; D. E. Cloyd, Cloquet.

Financial and Business Executive Board—R. E. Denfeld, Duluth; A. W. Rankin, Minneapolis; Miss Gertrude C. Ellis, Austin.

PURPOSES OF CHILD STUDY AND OF OUR ASSOCIATION.

Children have always been studied more or less by parents and teachers but not until recently have they been studied by scientists or in a scientific way. Our association and similar ones in other states aim to increase the interest in child study, awaken an appreciation of its importance and direct it in such a way that it will be more systematic, more scientific and more sympathetic.

The purpose most prominent in the minds of parents and teachers in the study of a child or a group of children is that they may understand them better, know how to deal with them more successfully and how to more wisely guard their physical, intellectual, emotional, volitional and moral development. The association recognizes this, and the chief aim of this pamphlet is to offer suggestions that will help parents and teachers attain these objects.

Scientists who study children have another purpose in view. A scientist is trying to discover general truths about children. He is not trying to discover the peculiar characteristics of a child which he wishes to influence but to find out what is true of all children, or of children of certain ages under certain conditions. He wants to learn these truths either because of his love of truth and desire to know all that can be known about children, just as other scientists wish to find out all they can about plants and animals, or else, because he wishes to get a basis for some other science, as that of education. The latter is most frequently the purpose of the scientific study of children, for it is now pretty generally recognized by thoughtful educators that few of the educational questions now under discussion as to courses of study, methods of teaching, etc., can be settled except by a more accurate determination of general truths as to the nature and development of children.

As has been said parents and teachers are usually most interested in the first aim of finding out particular truths about particular children with the expectation of making immediate use of such knowledge, yet they can gain their own ends better by learning what has already been found out about children in general and it is also possible for them to supply the specialist seeking for general truth with valuable facts which he can get in no other way. Parents and teachers should therefore not only study children for their own purposes, but should assist as much as possible in procuring data for specialists. It is also profitable for teachers occasionally to tabulate the results of some study of their school and make generalization as to children of a certain age, sex or class. It will have a broadening effect on the teacher and make it possible for her to more intelligently judge of the ability and characteristics of an individual pupil as compared with the average. Parents will also be profited by a comparison of their own observations with those of others and with generalizations that have been made.

In preparing the suggestions and outlines in this pamphlet the second or scientific purpose of child study has been kept in mind as well as the first and the interests of parents as well as those of teachers have been considered. Some of the observations and tests will be of most value in getting data for the establishment of general truths, others will have their principal value in what is learned in making the observation or test while some will be valuable for both purposes. Some of the suggestions are best suited for the teacher, others for parents, and all persons using the suggestions should consider carefully the purpose of the set of suggestions they are about to use and the conditions under which they can best be carried out. It is hoped that all members will cooperate in the attainment of both purposes of child study, sending any data they collect to the secretary or other designated person and correspond freely with him as to the best means of carrying out suggestions.

To study children successfully, a knowledge of psychological terms and familiarity with what has already been done in child study is helpful, though not absolutely necessary. *Caution* in making inferences and drawing positive conclusions and *patience* and *perseverance* to pursue the study till the truth is fully revealed, are still more important requisites for successful child study, but the only characteristic that is *absolutely essential*, is a *genuine sympathetic interest* in children. Let no one therefore attempt to carry out any of these suggestions in any other spirit. If any of the studies are made as matters of mere curiosities or amusement the children will detect it and the result will be valueless and perhaps injurious.

HEREDITY AND HOME INFLUENCES.

The teacher should take a personal interest in each pupil and seek to understand him by studying his hereditary tendencies and the influences outside of school that are affecting his development. The following facts are generally significant and can usually be learned by an observant, tactful teacher from incidental observation and conversation with pupils, from tests suggested in other parts of this pamphlet and from personal conversation with parents, who, if approached in the right spirit will take pleasure in talking about the characteristics of their children. In sending reports to the secretary or other designated person, of observations or tests, the age and sex of the pupils should always be given and in most cases it would be helpful to send some or all of the other facts suggested below. Name is not necessary.

Age of child—Sex—Number of brothers and sisters—Order in which child comes (counting oldest as first)—Nationality of father of mother of grandparents if known—Color of hair and eyes of father of mother - Size and build of father—of mother - Color of hair and eyes of child—Size (for age) and build of child Has father or mother, or grand-parents any marked physical or mental peculiarity and if so is it shown by the child? - If so, is it certainly inherited or may it be the result of imitations? —Has the child any peculiarity such as exceptional temper good or bad, or any unusual bodily or mental power or defect which causes him to be treated differently from what he would otherwise be by parents or associates?—Is the child's health good now? Has he ever had any serious illness?—What?

—How early did he learn to walk?—to talk?—At what age did he start to school?—Record anything remembered by child or parents as to early impressions and experiences especially those of his first term of school—Has he disliked school at any time and if so at what age and under what circumstances?—What is the degree of education of father?—of mother?—What is the occupation of the father?—What as to the kind and amount of reading matter in the home?—What as to the kind and amount of reading done by the child?—What kind of company has and does the child keep?—Is he leader or follower?—What does he do outside of school?—What are his favorite games?—What plans has he had or does he have now as to what he will do when grown?—Has his life been spent in country, village or city, and has he taken any long journeys?

HABIT.

Education is the process of forming habits of movement, thought, feeling and action. The teacher should, therefore, observe closely the effects of all general school exercises and rules and of all methods of study and recitation upon the habits of the school as a whole and upon each individual, and parents should make corresponding observations in the home. It should be remembered that a habit is an acquired tendency to do a certain thing under certain conditions and the exact conditions, both external and internal, under which the habit being studied is performed and the effects of changing those conditions should be carefully noted. One can study the habits of children much more intelligently and sympathetically if he first observes his own habits and tries breaking one or two of them, such as the pronunciation of a word, the use of a certain phrase, the taking of a certain route between two places, the order in which shoes or other articles of clothing are put on, the place in which some article of common use is put. Since so many habits originate in imitation, the outlines given below include suggestions bearing upon that as well as upon habit. If it is thought best children may be given an object-lesson on the power of habit by asking them to do something they do every day in a different way from what they are used to doing it. The outline is prepared for teachers but much of it can be used by parents with slight changes.

I.

1. Look for instances of imitation of teacher in voice, language, gesture, expression of face, attitude, ways of doing things and any mental or moral characteristic.

2. Note similar imitations of classmates and other persons and imitations of what has been read about.

3. Note whether the imitations are unconscious or intentional and persistent.

4. Give special attention to those that are liable to lead to the formation of good or bad habits of conduct and to those that are liable to help or hinder progress in the subject being studied.

5. Notice whether in any case the tendency to imitate is so strong as to prevent originality or so weak as to retard the formation of desirable habits.

II.

1. Note whether there are any habits common to the class as a whole or to nearly all of its members that interfere with good order and successful work during the recitation.

2. Notice what efforts, if any, are made to change those habits by the teacher and the effects of such efforts.

III.

1. Select one or more pupils for special study and note down all the attitudes, movements, phrases and actions that seem to be characteristic and more or less habitual.

2. Note especially habits that are commendable and those that interfere with the pupil's best and most rapid development.

3. Determine the origin of as many of the habits as possible.

4. Notice at what time of the day and under what circumstances the undesirable habits manifest themselves.

5. Note any change in the habits that seem to be taking place and especially the effects of the efforts of the teacher to modify them.

6. Discover, if you can, whether there is any one trait or habit that is the principal one and at bottom the cause of all the others.

7. State what means you think should be used to correct bad habits and preserve good ones in the pupils studied.

8. Note what habits of studying or doing things are being formed by the pupils in each subject studied that will be of advantage or disadvantage to them.

ATTENTION.

It is evident to everyone who has given the matter thought that time spent in talking to inattentive pupils is largely if not wholly wasted. The pupil also who fails to concentrate his attention during the study period learns little or nothing. It is important therefore that every teacher should be familiar with the signs and causes of attention and inattention that she may waste no time in giving instructions or directions to inattentive pupils. The ability to read the signs of attention, determine the causes, and apply the right nutriment or remedy can only be gained by practice. The following outline prepared by our former secretary L. H. Galbreath, will be found helpful in guiding such practice.

A STUDY OF ATTENTION IN CLASS WORK.

1. Signs of attention.

(a) How is attention to class work manifested, in bodily attitude, in actions, in questions, in answers, in reproductions or in voluntary participation? What help may come from this study?

(b) Can you find any signs peculiar to individuals? What manifestations are very general? What help may come from a knowledge of the peculiarities of attention?

(c) What variations in signs are discoverable in relation to time of day, to subject, to method, or to attitude of teacher?

2. Condition of attention.

(a) Are the conditions of *heat, light, atmosphere, seating* and of *seeing* and *hearing* in class work conducive to good attention? In what cases not?

(b) Are the *physical* conditions of the child's body with respect to health, degree of fatigue and muscular activity and experience conducive to attention? In what cases not?

(c) What *social events* or experiences at home in school or in the neighborhood perceptibly affect the attention to school room duties?

(d) How is attention conditioned by *previous study* in school or out of school as in reading, travel and the like?

3. Power of attention.

(a) What difference can you note in your children's *ability* to *grasp* thought? Can they attend equally well to matters of difficult interpretation?

(b) What differences in *intensity* are discernible? Is this difference noticeable in all subjects? Does it vary with the time of day?

(c) Is there a *difference* in the *rapidity* of attending to the matter of instruction? What variation is found in this?

(d) Can you find any peculiarities in attention in your pupils due to "eye-mindedness" or "ear-mindedness" or other special mental type?

4. Stimuli to attention.

(a) What external influences are operating to affect the pupil's attention either in direction or intensity?

(b) Through what senses is he receiving stimuli?

(c) What of these are subject to control by teacher and what not?

PERCEPTION AND APPERCEPTION.

Observation may be made upon perception incidentally outside of school work, and in school work whenever the pupils are studying oral or visual words, objects, pictures or maps, and upon apperception in connection with almost every subject. When the work of a class requires visual or auditory perception the teacher should note whether the external conditions of light, angle of vision, and distances are favorable for all the pupils to see or hear what is being presented and whether the internal condition of attention is also present. In every lesson she should ask herself "What knowledge does the class already have that they can use in understanding what is being studied?" And should notice whether they recall and use most pleasureably knowledge gained, (1) from personal experience, (2) from reading or hearsay, or (3) from the study of this or other subjects in school.

In observing an individual pupil, the condition of his sight and hearing with reference to where he sits should be considered, then the teacher should try to form a judgment as to the quickness and accuracy with which he perceives as compared with other pupils and to determine how far good or poor perception in these respects is due to apperceptive knowledge. It will be interesting also to note the characteristics of the pupil's perception as to classes of objects he observes or qualities noticed first, whether it is better in visual or auditory perception, whether he notices essential or non-essential qualities and whether he seems most interested in beauty, use or peculiarities of objects.

IMAGINATION.

In reading, history, geography and arithmetic, objects not present to the senses are frequently named and the ideas the children gain depend upon the clearness and accuracy of the images suggested by the words and the power the pupils have of combining them in the right way. The teacher, therefore, should always in connection with such exercises ask herself what images need to be formed and what basis in sense perception the pupils probably have for forming the correct images and how much power of making the proper combination they probably possess. The language used by pupils in reciting and their responses either in words or drawings to the question as to just how they have represented the object or scene (e. g. a banana tree or the battle of Trenton) in their own minds are some ways in which an observant teacher can find out how pupils are using their imaginations.

In studying individual children the teacher will find that some have better reproductive imaginations than others, i. e. can reproduce in their minds more vividly and accurately their past sense impressions; some have better constructive imagination i. e. can modify their images by enlarging them or by putting together images of what they have perceived according to directions so as to form images of what they have not seen, while still others have more of a creative imagination i. e. have the tendency to modify and combine images according to their own notions. The latter kind of imagination is shown especially in play, and original drawing and story writing. It will also be found that a large proportion use visual rather than auditory or other images. A knowledge of these facts will enable the teacher to more intelligently instruct children and to give each one the training most needed.

MEMORY.

In studying memory the teacher should seek especially to discover what kinds of mental images are most used and what kind of groupings and associations are most helpful. The kind of images most used is of special importance in spelling and can often be determined by noticing the kind of mistakes made in spelling words. Special tests given elsewhere and observations as to whether what is given orally or what is read silently is remembered best and how much memory is assisted by writing or repeating will help to determine whether children are the visual, auditory or motor type.

As to association the teacher should note how much better pupils remember facts that are grouped than those given haphazard, and what kind of grouping seems most favorable to memory also as to how much memory is helped by association with objects, pictures, word pictures, diagrams, or with any group of facts already known. She should also notice how far in reproducing, pupils follow the order in which the facts were given and when they vary the order whether any other order is substituted. The amount that pupils can best learn at one time and the frequency of review required should also receive watchful attention. Individual peculiarities in all these respects as to kind of facts best remembered and permanency of memory should be noted.

CONCEPTION AND REASONING.

In observing evidences of these higher intellectual processes the way in which words are used, defined and truths applied should be noted, for the meaning attached to a word constitutes one's concept, and the forming of general truths and the application of them involve reasoning. The teacher should continually watch to see that pupils are not getting wrong ideas of things about which they are studying, and to see that they really have the right idea of words supposed to be familiar. In determining just what their ideas are and how to correct them, it will be well for the teacher to consider whether the idea has probably been gotten (a) from direct experience (b) from description or definition or (c) by inference from the way in which the word is used in connection with other words whose meaning is known. In trying to give pupils a general notion or concept (for example what a prime number or an adverb is), they should not only learn the characteristics or the definition but should be tested as to their ability to recognize the characteristics in concrete examples. In the attempts of pupils to thus recognize or classify, the teacher should notice whether mistakes are due to imperfect knowledge of the characteristics of the class or to the lack of discrimination of the particular characteristics of what is being classified and then act accordingly.

In studying reasoning the teacher should notice how many examples are required before different pupils make a generalization and how ready they are to apply a general truth they have learned. If mistakes are made note what likeness the pupil has probably siezed upon and whether mistakes are due (a) to choosing wrong characteristics (b) imperfect discrimination of characteristics (c) lack of knowledge of the general truth to be applied (d) lack of power of attention to keep several ideas in mind till a conclusion can be reached.

GENERAL OUTLINE FOR RECORDING JUDGMENTS AS TO A CHILD'S INTELLECTUAL ABILITY AND PECULIARITIES.

Name—   Age—   Sex—   Nationality—
Other significant facts. (See "Heredity and Home Influences.")

ATTENTION.
    Habit of attention as to degree—
        In class.
        When studying.
    Power of attention—
        As to time he can attend.
        As to readiness with which he can change.
        As to the number of things he can keep in mind at once without confusion.
    Characteristics of attention—
        Are there any signs of attention peculiar to himself which a teacher should know?
        Are there any subjects or conditions in which he shows marked attention or inattention?

PERCEPTION AND APPERCEPTION.
    Perfectness of sense organs.
    Quickness of perception.
    Accuracy of perception.
    Peculiarities of perception.
    Apperceptive knowledge—
        Amount.
        Kind.
        Readiness in using.

IMAGINATION.
    Reproductive—
        Vividness.
        Accuracy.
        Kind of image most used.
    Constructive—
        Readiness.
        Accuracy.

Creative—
> Power.
> Does tendency to create interfere with accuracy of perception or construction or memory?
> Is imagination aesthetic, intellectual or inventive?

MEMORY.
> Kind of image most used.
> Which is remembered best, thought or words?
> Power of memory—
>> In daily lessons.
>> In review.
> Does he often recall facts without knowing where they belong?
> Does he often recognize as correct what he was unable to recall?
> Is his memory for any kind of facts especially good or poor?
> Does he associate facts in a systematic way?

CONCEPTION AND REASONING.
> Concepts—
>> Number.
>> Perfectness.
>> In what lines best?
> Reasoning—
>> Ability to follow reasoning.
>> Tendency to reason for himself.
>> Tendency to generalize.
>> Tendency to apply general truths.
>> Accuracy of reasoning.
>> Is reasoning especially good or poor in any subject?

The above gives a brief form for recording the results of a study of individual children. In all cases the child should be compared with others of his class and age, and adjectives should indicate whether he is average, or above or below average, little or much. The teacher will find the making out of a few such reports as this profitable in giving definiteness to her observations and they will be of much more value to the teacher to whom the pupil next goes than a mere record of standing. Such reports would also be very valuable to a superintendent in settling difficult cases of promotion. The following form quoted from Communication XI may also be found valuable.

ATTEMPTED IMPROVEMENT OF A SCHOOL AND OF A PUPIL.

I.

If at the beginning of your school this year, or at any time since, you found the school as a whole or any class as a whole, in an unsatisfactory state, either as regards conduct or scholarship in any particular study, please describe as fully and clearly as possible, giving concrete illustrations, (*a*) the condition; (*b*) the cause of the condition; (*c*) the means you have taken to correct it; (*d*) the results.

II.

Describe any pupil who has given you trouble, either as regards behavior or learning, covering the following points:

1. Age and sex of child.
2. Nationality and education of the parents, and any other significant facts about the home surroundings of the child.
3. Condition of the child as regards physical peculiarities or defects, particularly those of sense organs or movements, (describe any means you have used to determine perfectness of eye or ear).
4. Mental peculiarities that you have noted.
5. A full account of the undesirable actions or the defects in scholarship which you wish to correct.
6. What you have found to be the probable cause of his or her present condition.
7. What you have done to remedy the defect.
8. Results of the various means used, and the present condition of the child.

A detailed description of one case is better than a general description of many, and it is especially important that the facts upon which your opinions are founded should be given definitely.

SPECIAL STUDIES AND TESTS.

With the exercise of a little tact a teacher can profitably use many of the suggestions outlined below as a means of getting better acquainted with her pupils and in some instances of collecting valuable data. They can be used as language lesson or as tests, or games in general exercises, being introduced by a few remarks calculated to rouse an interest in the subject and lead them to express themselves freely and frankly, or do their best and most rapid work as the test may require.

AUTOBIOGRAPHY.

In a language lesson pupils may be told what an autobiography is, then told to write one. If an outline is given them the following will serve.

1. Name, age and place of birth and occupation of father.
2. Earliest recollections.
3. Places lived in and journeys taken.
4. Studies and school experiences.
5. Other interesting experiences and facts.

In connection with the above or at another time the following subject and outline may be given.

PLEASANT THINGS TO DO.

1. What I like to do now in the way of work, play or reading.
2. What I would like to do sometime.

MY EXPERIENCES WITH MONEY.

I. *Getting money.*

1. Experiences in earning money. what was done, when, why, and how many times.
2. Experiences in receiving money as a gift or allowance; from whom, under what circumstances.
3. How I should like to get money when grown and why: in what business, and which would be better, to work for money or to have it given to one without working?

II. *Saving money.*

Experiences in saving money; where it was kept, how long, for what purpose and was it finally spent for that purpose?

III. *Spending money.*

1. Description of different ways in which it has been spent.
2. What I would do with the money if I had a chance to get fifty cents a day for a month.
3. Which would be most desirable, and why, to have clothes, books and playthings bought by parents or to receive money to buy them?
4. Which would be best, to have five dollars to-day, ten a year from now or one hundred, ten years from now?

CHILDREN'S READING.

1. Give the names of all papers or magazines that you read regularly or hear read, stating which one you like best and why.
2. State as accurately as you can the number of books that you have read outside of school since the beginning of this school year. How many of these did you read more than once or had you read before?
3. Give the names of as many books that you read this year as you can.
4. State which one you like best and why.
5. Which of your school subjects do you like best and for what reason if you know?

Questions similar to the above should be asked every year.

QUESTIONS ABOUT LAST YEAR'S WORK.

Any teacher especially one who knows what her pupils had last year will have a flood of light thrown upon children's interests and memory, and upon the question of what subjects and methods are most impressive by asking questions in regard to last year's work, such as the following, and by giving them a set or two of last year's examination questions.

What did you study about last year in geography?

Name some of the "pieces" you read in your reader last year and give all you can remember about one of them.

TEST OF ACCURACY OF MENTAL IMAGES AND OF INCIDENTAL ATTENTION AND MEMORY.

1. Without measuring, draw a horizontal line one inch long and another five inches.

2. State in inches how high and how far across a vessel must be to hold a quart of milk.

3. Draw lines to represent the actual height and distance across of the larger size of fruit and vegetable cans usually sold in groceries.

4. State in inches the size a vessel must be to hold a gallon.

5. State in feet the distance between the tracks made by wagon wheels.

6. Which way do the seeds of an apple point?

7. Which leave out first in the spring, willows or oaks? Which lose their leaves first?

8. How many legs and how many wings has a fly?

9. How much does a brick weigh?

10. How long has it been since the World's Fair?

11. Ask how long since some recent event known to all and not definitely associated with an announced date.

12. Ask the number of panes of glass in some window all have seen frequently.

13. Ask the distance between two well known objects.

14. Ask the number of houses on a well known street for a block or two.

15. Have the pupils sit quietly with hands folded then give a signal and after the lapse of a minute another, then ask how long the time has been.

TEST OF IMAGINATION AND REASONING.

1. If you were to walk directly west five miles how far would you be from the schoolhouse?

2. Two men six miles apart walked directly toward each other, one walking two miles and the other three: How far apart were they then?

3. Two men were three miles apart on a north and south line and one walked north two miles and the other south three miles: How far apart were they then?

4. Two men on an east and west line were four miles apart and they both walked west, the west one three miles and the east one two miles: How far apart were they then?

5. If it is worth sixty cents to saw a cord of wood making two pieces of each stick what will it be worth to saw it making three pieces of each stick?

6. "If you were shipwrecked on a island of the sea and you found in one corner of the island an old house of logs and part of an old wooden boat with broken arrows in the bottom of it, what would these things tell you?"

The children should be given plenty of time to write all they want to on the above story taken from Barnes' "Studies in Education." The problems can be given in lower grades as well as higher and perhaps receive equally as many correct answers.

TESTS OF DISCRIMINATION.

The simplest test of discrimination is to judge which is the larger of two nearly equal lines drawn, or held slanting one to the right and the other to the left, or to draw lines equal to those shown, or to bisect narrow slips of paper laid in a certain position. The simplest color test is to have them select a color from a number of colors like one shown. Auditory discrimination may be tested by having the pupils tell which of two sounds produced by dropping weights from slightly different heights is the louder, or which of two notes sounded on an instrument is the higher.

Discrimination and perception may be tested by having pupils try to recognize various objects by touch, taste, smell or sound. Such tests may be a sort of a game for little folks in general exercises with advantage to both pupils and teacher. The teacher should notice what relation exists between power of discrimination and mental ability as shown in the other work of the school.

TESTS OF MENTAL AND MOTOR QUICKNESS.

1. Have pupils make vertical marks as rapidly as possible for ten seconds.

2. Have them write figures beginning with 1 and writing in order as rapidly as possible.

3. Have them write numbers beginning with 2 and counting by twos.

1. The same as in 3, but beginning with one.
5. The same as 3 and 4 with higher numbers.

Tests similar to this should be made in connection with all drill work in arithmetic as a means of measuring the rate of progress. The teacher should notice what relation there is between quickness and accuracy in movement and quickness and accuracy in mental operations.

Older pupils may be tested as to mental quickness and also as to peculiarity of association by having them write words in columns as fast as they can think of them for three or five minutes.

MEMORY AND MENTAL IMAGE TEST.

The following prepared by Miss Isabel Lawrence and sent out as Communication VI can be used both as a memory test and as a means of determining the kind of images most used by pupils:

Make a list of eight or ten familiar monosyllables, so arranged as to avoid association.

1. One list marked "A" presented, one word at a time, on cards so that each is clearly seen. When the last word is withdrawn, the pupils write them on a paper marked "Sight A."

2. Pupils now listen to another list of the same number of words marked "B." After these words have been pronounced distinctly in succession, the pupils write them on a paper marked "Sound B."

3. Take the same list as in "2," or the one marked "B," vary the order, and present to sight as list "A" was presented in "1." Pupils write them on a paper marked "Sight B."

4. Take the same list as in "1," list "A," vary this in order, and pronounce as in "2." Pupils write this list on a paper marked "Sound A."

The papers should be collected after each exercise.

Caution: All pupils should hear and see distinctly. The purpose of the test is not to detect defective eye-sight or hearing. Cards similar to those to be used should be presented before the test. If pupils cannot see or hear distinctly, have them change their seats to places where they can.

A report like the following can be made. Notice that a column is left for ear and eye tests which may be correlated with this.

Name of pupil	John Smith
Grade	Fourth
Age	10
Total number of words given	20
*Total number reproduced in sight test	7
Total number reproduced in hearing test	18
Words substituted in sight test	Fiend
Words for which substituted	Friend
Words substituted in hearing test	
Words for which substituted	
†Sense test,—sight	8 ft. 7 in.
‡Sense test,—hearing	10 ft. 5 in.
Scholarship: Reading	Very Poor
Spelling	Poor
Observation,—nature study	Good
Arithmetic	Very Good

*A word should be counted as reproduced when it is recognizable as the word presented, even though it be misspelled.
†Sense tests: Sight—distance at which letters one-half inch long are distinguished.
‡Sense tests: Hearing—distance at which the ticking of a watch is heard.

Several important pedagogical questions may receive light if extensive Child Study be undertaken in this direction, and continued for a number of years. These questions are largely in the realm of language, and will govern the method of giving children clear and distinct percepts of words, a process so important to ready reading, correct spelling, and possibly ready speaking. Possibly experiment may extend beyond the limit of words, but I confine myself to them in the following questions suggested for solution:

1. Are there ear-minded people who take in words by sound, even though they see them?

2. Are there eye-minded people who take in words by sight, even though they only hear them?

3. If "1" and "2" should be answered affirmatively, is this characteristic due to education? Is it inherited? Is it due to defects of sight or hearing? Can we, as Balliet thinks, make children ear-minded or eye-minded at will?

To answer the last question, "3," tests of sight and hearing which are usually used in Child Study should be correlated with these tests.

4. Do the majority of pupils take in words by both methods equally well? See Articles of Eye and Ear Mindedness by

Prof. Bryan, University of Indiana, p. 779. Pro. N. E. A., 1893. Also Supt. Balliet's Address, p. 756.

5. Can the child who is ear-minded become eye-minded,— and vice versa?

6. If it is possible to change ear-minded pupils to eye-minded, is it desirable?

Shall we adapt our methods of teaching so as to reach the ear-minded pupil through hearing? Shall we teach him to study by methods which appeal to the ear, while we use the reverse process with the eye-minded? Or shall we try to train ear-minded pupils to acquire by the eye?

7. Which class, ear-minded or eye-minded, include the best readers and spellers? Prof. Bryan, Supt. Balliet and Dr. Granville differ in their answers to these questions. Is demonstration possible?

It is suggested that at least three tests should be made of each child, one at least with the child separated from his class. These tests are still better if made by different teachers.

Slight differences in the number of words should be disregarded. If a pupil tested several times invariably reproduces four or more words more by sound than by sight, or if his substitutions are such as would naturally take place if one heard the word in taking in the impression, he may be safely pointed out as ear-minded. Similar conditions may prove a pupil eye-minded.

Tests repeated for successsive years may prove whether pupils change in this respect.

SOME SUGGESTIONS FOR OBSERVATIONS BY PARENTS.

OBSERVATION ON INFANTS AND YOUNG CHILDREN.

1. *Taste.* When does the child come to like salt or sour and does it come to like bitter at all or naturally? Describe the substances used and the circumstances under which these tastes first became agreeable. (The question about bitter will have much bearing on the hygiene and ethics of tobacco and bitter stimulating drinks.) In experiments the solid or liquid substances need not be swallowed but placed on the tongue till some reaction is noted then wiped or rinsed off.

2. *Color.* When does the child notice colors? Which colors first? Tested with its choice of books of different bindings or with Bradley or Prang color papers what are its two or three preferred colors? Does it seem to dislike any or merely not notice them?

3. *Memory.* Note some average sample of memory. Are more memories connected with pleasurable or painful things? Are the longest memories about painful or pleasurable things?

4. *Association.* Note the time and describe the first cases of acquired association, e. g. movements showing expectation of the bottle with the putting of a cloth under the chin or with the sight of a bottle filled or empty, etc.

5. *Shame* and *Cleanliness.* Note time and describe first cases. Do they seem to you instinctive in the children or acquired?

6. *Reasoning.* Some of the first cases of what seem to you reasoning. More complicated ones up to school age.

The above suggestions were prepared by Prof. H. Gale, of the University of Minnesota, Minneapolis, and persons making any of the above observations will do a great favor by sending their results to him.

SUGGESTIONS FOR THE STUDY OF LANGUAGE DEVELOPMENT.

The development of language and of thought also can best be studied by observing and recording children's vocabularies during the period from one to four years when they are learning to use language and have not yet so many words that it is almost impossible to keep a record of new ones. This is a study which it is possible for every parent to make to a greater or less extent and secure data that will have at least some scientific value.

The development of speech in children may be studied either as a process of learning to make certain series of movement i. e., those of the vocal apparatus involved in pronouncing words or as a process of thought development in which the concept or classifications adopted by people generally are learned by the child. The more knowledge one has of these two processes the more intelligently they can study and record language development, yet without such knowledge a study and record of some value may be made.

The method used may be that of keeping pencil and paper at hand and recording every new word as it is used or that of making a special study of the child's vocabulary at regular intervals of from one to six months and recording all the words used at that time. In making records observe the following points and send the vocabularies to the secretary, who is collecting as many vocabularies as possible, especially of children about two years of age.

1. Record words that are used by the child with a distinct meaning rather than words merely repeated after some one, or words understood but not spoken by the child himself, (though separate lists of the last two classes of words may be kept if desired).

2. Indicate (*a*) how each word is pronounced, if there is any peculiarity of pronunciation, (*b*) what part of speech the word is, as used by the child, (*c*) the meaning the child attaches to the word, if it differs in any way from the ordinary meaning.

3. Record all words including names and different forms of the same word as "be", "am", "walk", "walked".

4. Keep a record of characteristic phrases and sentences used by the child at different ages.

5. Send with the vocabulary, (*a*) a statement of the method of recording it, (*b*) of the policy pursued as regards teaching the child words either directly or indirectly by refusing to supply wants not expressed in words, (*c*) the principal facts mentioned under Heredity and Home Influences, especially those with regard to brothers and sisters and other companions.

SUGGESTIONS FOR PARENTS' AND TEACHERS' MEETINGS.

If, in every school district in city, village and country parents and teachers would meet once a month and frankly discuss the conditions most favorable to the best development of children, there would be a greater improvement in school and home management of children during the next year than there has ever been in any previous ten years. The following is the plan for organizing such meetings adopted in Detroit: "It was proposed to organize a league in each school district of the city of which every woman in it, regardless of creed, color, nationality or environment should be asked to become a member. It was decided to have the meetings of those leagues held in the school buildings once every month, after the regular work for the day was over. At each of these meetings which were to be presided over by a regularly elected principal (usually the principal of the school), there were to be free discussions among the mothers and teachers upon the topics best suited to aid in the proper development of the child." The following are some of the topics suggested for discussion by Mrs. Eliza Bert Gamble, of Detroit.

DISCIPLINE.

1. (*a*) Do you think corporal punishment ever necessary?

(*b*) If so, do you think it a good means of punishment for all children?

(*c*) Has it an injurious effect upon nervous children, and in what way?

(*d*) Does it tend to make children cowardly or rebellious, and has it a hardening effect on some children, especially those over ten years of age?

2. (*a*) Is it not advisable to punish children by depriving them of meals, or by putting them in solitary confinement?

3. (*a*) Should the parent, upon receipt of complaint from the teacher, punish the child other than by reproof?

(*b*) It is not advisable for the mother to confer with the teacher upon receiving such complaint?

4. (*a*) If a child realizes that he will receive severe punishment, such as beating, etc., for childish carelessness, does such knowledge tend to make him deceitful and incline him to conceal his faults from his parents and teachers, and take refuge in untruthfulness to avoid punishment?

(*b*) Is the mother or teacher ever justified in deceiving a child?

(*c*) Should the rights of the child be regarded and his ideas respected?

(*d*) How would you teach children to respect the rights of others?

5. (*a*) In cases of nervous, timid children, will the fear of punishment incline to further deceit?

(*b*) Have you observed the effect of fear upon the child when expecting punishment?

(*c*) Do children under five understand the principles of truthfulness?

(d) How would you teach truthfulness to a very young child?

6. (a) How would you deal with an ill-tempered child?
(b) What are the possible physical causes of ill-temper?
(c) What are the possible mental causes of ill-temper?
(d) When a child is subject to violent spells of passion, would you consult a physician?
(e) Can we distinguish easily between a temper that will not be controlled, the child being headstrong and self-willed, and a temper which results from excitement, nervous irritability, or over-study, and which he cannot control until these conditions are removed?
(f) To what extent should we consider heredity in children?

7. (a) Is it well to rebuke a child frequently for restlessness, often caused by nervous temperament, which must have an outlet, or by an over-worked condition of mind or body?
(b) Have you observed that severe checking of such restlessness often produces serious disorders, such as St. Vitus's dance, etc.?
(c) What do you think is the best method of checking restlessness?
(d) Should a child be punished for restlessness?

8. (a) How can we most effectually deal with habits of greediness, untidiness, indolence and disobedience in children from five to nine and from nine to sixteen years of age?

9. (a) Has confidence in the tenderness of the mother, or fear of the severity of the father the greater influence on the child?
(b) Do you not think it wiser to prevent the forming of bad habits by the child than to punish him after such habits are formed?
(c) How would you try to prevent the boy from learning objectionable and injurious habits, for instance, smoking, chewing tobacco, using profane language and slang, reading pernicious literature, and associating with evil companions?
(d) How would you teach a child self-control, and a proper regard for the rights of others?

RECREATION AND LITERATURE.

RECREATION.

1. (*a*) How many hours should children aged from five to nine, and from nine to fifteen, respectively, play daily.

2. (*a*) What ought we to guard against when allowing delicate children to join with robust children in outdoor games?

(*b*) When we notice that a child loses breath quickly and becomes pale after violent exercise, to what cause should we attribute these conditions?

(*c*) Under these conditions is it necessary to consult a physician?

3. (*a*) Which are the healthiest outdoor games?

(*b*) Which are objectionable?

(*c*) What games do girls enjoy most in the home, and which do boys prefer?

4. (*a*) Do you approve the plan (when possible) of having in the home a pleasant, cheerful room set apart as a playroom?

(*b*) What should this room contain?

5. (*a*) What kind of games should nervous children play?

(*b*) What kind should be discouraged?

(*c*) Have you noticed that in the case of nervous children the playing or games requiring the exercise of mental powers, late in the evening, has a tendency to induce wakefulness and dreaming?

(*d*) Ought children to be discouraged from playing games in which ghosts, goblins, etc., are represented?

6. (*a*) Will you give some suggestions for amusing children between the ages of 6 to 10, on stormy days, or during convalescence?

(*b*) Do you think that the preference shown by children for certain occupations and games indicates the tendency of the mind toward certain trades or professions?

(*c*) Should this be encouraged in every way possible?

7. (*a*) What do you think of such recreation as base-ball, foot-ball and tennis?

(*b*) Should girls play them?

LITERATURE.

1. (*a*) What style of literature ought to be put in the hands of girls and boys aged, respectively. from six to ten and from ten to sixteen?

2. (*a*) Is the reading of fairy tales desirable as tending to develop the child's imagination?

(*b*) Are tales of adventure, if well written and of wholesome morality, injurious to children?

(*c*) To what extent should the child's reading be confined to story-books?

3. (*a*) At what age would you permit novel reading?

(*b*) Would you make any exceptions in favor of Dickins, Scott, or Thackeray?

(*c*) Should children be encouraged to read the daily newspapers?

4. (*a*) Should we endeavor to cultivate a taste for poetry in the child; if so, how should it be done?

(*b*) What influence has good poetry upon the child's literary taste and on his mind?

(*c*) Considering the age of the child, is the reading of the best poets, even when a little beyond his comprehension, better than ordinary rhymes?

5. (*a*) How can we guard against the growth of a taste for trashy or bad books?

(*b*) Is it well to explain to the child why certain books are pernicious in their tendency, or simply, so far as possible, to keep such books out of his way.

6. (*a*) Is it well to encourage children to collect books and to have a personal pride in the possession of good works, or should they depend wholly on public libraries?

(*b*) Should children, from an early age, be taught to take good care of books?

7. (*a*) How should a mother succeed in guiding the literary taste of her child?

PART II.

OUTLINE FOR THE STUDY OF THE EMOTIONS.

BY ISABEL LAWRENCE.

I. HAPPINESS OR UNHAPPINESS.

SUGGESTION FOR STUDY.

Record cases of children in your school who are often unhappy. Find out if they are unhappy at home.

How long has this continued?

Search for causes; (*a*) in heredity; (*b*) in environment; (*c*) sensitiveness; (*d*) fatigue; (*e*) disease; (*f*) fears, etc.

Dr. Warner says, in "How to Study Children," that he has frequently found a settled, anxious expression on the faces of young children, and after trying in vain to find out the reason from the parents, he has gained the child's confidence and drawn out its stories of terrors in darkness, visions, or mental trouble which the little child would not speak of before, because it was not understood.

READING.

1. *Questionaire* on Crying and Laughing, Dr. G. Stanley Hall. Trans. Ill. Soc., Vol. I. No. 3, or Topical Syllabi for '94. '95.

2. The Children, How to Study them. Dr. Francis Warner.

II. FEAR.

SUGGESTION FOR STUDY.

Ask children what they most fear. Have them describe it to you, or, as **Dr.** Colin A. Scott has suggested, have them draw or paint it for you.

READING.

1. *Questionaire* by Dr. G. Stanley Hall, on Fears in Childhood and Youth. Topical Syllabi for '94 and '95, Clark University. Also in Tran. Ill. Soc. of Child Study, Vol. I. No. 2.

2. Study of Fear—Dr. G. Stanley Hall. Am. Jour. of Psych., Vol. VIII. No. 2. This study is based on the above *questionaire*

3. Study of Fear. Pamphlet. Dr. Colin A. Scott, Chicago Normal School.

4. Wellesley College Psychological Studies. Pedagogical Seminary Vol. III. No. 2.

5. Stanford Studies in Education have the following articles relating to the subject: No. I. Fear in childhood—Agnes Sinclair Holbrook. No. II. Children and Ghosts—Louise Maitland. No. IV. A Study of Children's Superstitions—Clara Vastrovsky. No. V. Children's Attitude towards Ghosts—Louise Maitland.

6. Fear—Angelo Mosso. A book of 278 pages. Price $2.00. Longmans, Green & Co.

7. The Senses and the Will—W. Preyer. See pages 164-172.

8. The Infant Mind—W. Preyer. See pages 22-29.

9. The Children and How to Study Them—Warner. See page 58.

III. SOCIAL FEELINGS.

SUGGESTION FOR STUDY.

Note the groupings of your school at recess and intermissions.

Make a record of cases of strong attachments or enmities. Notice the domination of one child by another. Record the instances in which the child imitates his leader. Make a careful record of quarrels or fights.

Do not depend upon questioning the children. Questions may help occasionally if used with tact and indirectly, but on this topic they are more or less dangerous.

Reminiscence studies may be furnished by adults following these directions:

Describe in detail any case of liking or disliking any adult or playmate, which occurred in your own life before the age of sixteen. Give your age at the time, state how long the emotion lasted and the circumstances of change, if it ever altered.

READING.

Read autobiographies and note similar cases in them. Some interesting studies for instance may be found in:

1. My Schools and School Masters—Hugh Miller. See page 135, etc.

2. Childhood, Boyhood, and Youth—Count Tolstoi. A book of 244 pages. Thos. Y. Crowell & Co. See chapter XIX on Serozha Ivin.

3. A Day at Eton. 16 mo. pp. 184. C. W. Bardeen, Syracuse. Price $1.00.

4. Study Maggie's love for Tom in George Eliot's Mill on the Floss. Direct studies on this topic are:

5. *Questionaire* on "Affection and its Opposite States," by Dr. G. Stanley Hall. Topical Syllabi for '94 and '95.

6. *Questionaire* on "The Social Sense"—J. Mark Baldwin. Trans. Ill. Soc., Vol. I. No. 2.

7. *Questionaire* on Anger by Dr. G. Stanley Hall. Topical Syllabi for '94 and '95. Also in Trans. Ill. Soc., Vol. I. No. 3.

8. A Study of Anger, by Dr. Hall is soon to appear in either the Ped. Sem., or in the Am. Jour. of Psych.

9. Teasing and Bullying—A study by Frederick L. Burk. Ped. Sem., Vol. IV. No. 3.

10. What Determines Leadership in Children's Plays—Clara Vostrovsky. Stanford Studies in Education. No. 5.

11. Wellesley College Psychological Studies—Love and Hate. Ped. Sem. Vol. III. No. 2.

12. See pages 103 and 104 of Warner's. "The Children, How to Study Them."

IV. CHILDREN'S IDEALS.

This involves a study of Hopes, Ambitions, Æsthetic Feelings and Interests.

SUGGESTION FOR STUDY.

The following syllabus has been tested in several schools.

The questions, one or more at a time, are given to the older grades as composition exercise during school hours.

No suggestion or explanation should be given to the pupils. No pupil should ask for the spelling of a word, as experience proves that the word is sure to be adopted by other pupils who would not otherwise have expressed that idea.

Pupils of younger grades to whom writing is not yet a means of free expression, should be interviewed individually.

The papers on this subject may be sent to Miss Isabel Lawrence, Normal School, St. Cloud. Due credit will be given to all teachers helping in this study.

SYLLABUS.

If a fairy should promise to give you just what you wish, and to change you when you grow up, into just such a man or woman as you would like to become, what answers would you make to the following questions:

1. What do you choose as to personal appearance and dress? (Form for little children, how would you like to look and to dress?)

2. Describe the place in which you would like to live.

3. What do you wish to do when you grow up? Why?

4. What person that you ever heard or read about, do you wish to be like? Why?

Older grades who would not be interested in the idea of the fairy may be given the following preface:

Suppose that you could be, and could have whatever you wished for, what answer would you make to the following questions, etc.:

Let the *teacher*, write age, sex, and nationality of parents at the top of the paper. Number the answers to correspond with the questions. Write only on one side of the paper.

READING.

1. Preliminary Study of Children's Hopes—J. P. Taylor. Exhibit, No 18. Child Study Department of Education, New York.

2. Children's Ambitions—Hattie Mason Willard. Stanford Studies in Education. No. VII.

3. What Children Want to do when they are Men and Women—Prof. Chas. W. Thurber. Trans. Ill. Soc. Vol. II. No. 2. Complete report may be obtained of Prof. Thurber at the University of Chicago.

4. Answers to Questions on what do you want to do when you grow up, obtained from Kindergarten children Anne E. Allen. Trans. Ill. Soc. Vol. II. No. 2.

V. CHILDREN'S INTERESTS.

SUGGESTIONS FOR STUDY.

To find out the interests of children, try some of the following methods:

1. Ask children what certain common objects are. Note the elements which predominate in their descriptions. Binet, Earl Barnes, Shaw have made studies of this kind. See 1, 2 and 3, under the following reading.

Analyze children's original stories; their reproductions after some time has elapsed; or the stories which they like best. What elements predominate? See the study of stories in 8. Analyze the reading-matter used by the school to see if it corresponds to these discovered interests.

3. Tell the bare outline of some story in history, barely describe some place in geography, or perform some experiment in science, without comment. Let classes ask questions. Note what they wish to know about these things. Studies of this kind have been made in history by Mary Sheldon Barnes, and in nature study by Dr. Colin A. Scott. See 5 and 7.

READING.

1. A Study of Children's Interests Earl Barnes. Stanford Studies in Education No. VI.

2. Review of Binet's Study in Am. Jour. of Psych., Vol. III., p. 273.

3. A Comparative Study of Children's Interests—Edward R. Shaw. Child Study Monthly. July and Aug. '96.

4. Stanford Studies in Education have several reminiscent studies relating to this topic: No. VI. Children's Interest in Plants—Katherine A. Chandler. No. VI. Children's Collections—Earl Barnes. No. II. Memories of Things Read—Agnes Sinclair Holbrook.

5. The Historic Sense Among Children—Mary Sheldon Barnes. Stanford Studies in Education. No. II. and III.

6. Love of Nature as the Root of Teaching and Learning the Sciences—W. A. Hoyt. Ped. Sem. Vol. III. No. 2.

7. Study of Interest in Nature Study—Dr. Colin Scott. Chicago Normal School.

8. A Study of Children's Own Stories—Clara Vostrovsky. Stanford Studies in Education. No. I.

9. Study of a Child's Book—Ora Boring. Ped. Sem. Vol. II. p. 303.

10. Life of Washington—Louise Smythe. A reader for children, but really an experiment in study of children's interests.

PART III.

PRACTICAL SUGGESTIONS FOR THE STUDY OF THE PHYSICAL NATURE OF CHILDREN.

BY STUART H. ROWE, PH. D.

The practical achievements of Child Study, in as far as it has influenced the schoolroom, have been largely in the field of the child's physical nature. We have been proved guilty of ignorance, carelessness and neglect, and all over the country we are, at least, trying to show that that ignorance was not willful. Children formerly accused of stupidity, stubbornness and indolence, have been found to lack normal conditions. This child is lacking in keenness of sight, another in hearing. Some children are defective in motor ability, others have diseases which cause them to be easily fatigued. For some of these defects the school is found to be responsible. The design of this paper is to offer suggestions to any who would atone for the past by greater care for the future. The results of scientific investigation will be included wherever they are likely to be helpful.

SIGHT.

About twenty per cent. of the children in upper grades have some perceptible difficulty with the eye, which may be discovered by a careful test. The difficulty is usually myopia, or short-sightedness. Probably less than three per cent. of the children have that difficulty upon entering school. In fact, the young child's eye is far-sighted (hypermetropic), and does not become normal until about the seventh year. The causes of defective eyesight are poor light, fine print, bad position, i. e., holding the book too near or too far from the eye, tight neckwear, rubbing, disease, cigarette smoking, and unhealthy home conditions. The effect of school work is headache and a tired, nervous condition, making it hard for the child to attend successfully to his book or the blackboard, and the consequent unwillingness and inability to make the attempt for any but a very limited period. These manifestations will not be constant, but will show themselves with increasing frequency as the child advances in the grades. The after-school headache is another form. These are not sufficiently prominent at first and are too serious in their import as to the condition of the eye for us to wait for their appearance, before we find out about the condition of the eye. This is really a very simple matter, if the following directions are followed implicitly. Get Snellen's Test Types, by enclosing ten cents to Prof. Krohn, Psychological Laboratory of the University of Illinois, Champaign, Illinois, asking him to send you the Test Types. Hang the chart up in good light. Then, beginning not less than sixty feet from the chart, test the child's ability to read the type at that distance with each eye. Then advance to the next distance indicated on the chart, and try each eye at that distance, and so on. By waiting a moment between the tests for the two eyes, you will soon find out which eye sees better. After that always test the poorer eye first. Do not hurry the child and, if he tires, give him a rest before you finish. If he can see none of the letters at the required distances, find out what he can see; but usually the eye which does not see at that distance (if the light is good and the card clean) should be examined by a physician. This test is with regard to keen sightedness for blackboard work. To test for myopia (near sightedness) and astigmatism, send for the Test of Vision for Use in Schools, prepared by James W. Queen, 1010 Chestnut St., Philadelphia. The cost of this is twenty-five cents. The directions, which are very clear, will be found on the back of the card. If the directions are not understood, apply to any physician. Whenever visual imperfections are evident, urge the parents to have a physician examine and treat the case. Some children read with their books too close to their eyes. Such cases need your tests, and probably a physician's.

In searching for causes of eye difficulty, it is well first of all to investigate our schoolrooms to see if there is light enough. We are told that there should be one square foot of window for each square foot of floor surface; that this light should be unobstructed by other buildings or trees. It should come as nearly as possible over the left shoulder of the child and should come from one side of the room only The curtain should be raised from a roller fastened *below* the window (rather than the reverse, as is usual), in order that the child may under no circumstances have to face directly the bright light.

In most school rooms there are seats from which a part of the blackboard can not be seen. Do you know which they are in your room? Test the accuracy of your knowledge in this way. Divide off all the blackboard space in your room into sections of four or five feet, labeling them as you do so A, B, C, D, etc. Then make a map including each seat in the room, and go from seat to seat surveying all the blackboard space from each. Enter on your map the letter for each section of the board not seen clearly at each stopping place. Be careful to place your head in about the same position usually occupied by the child's. See what effect certain common positions of the curtain have. If a child cannot see where you can, test his eyes.

Our text-books have not always been guiltless in the print offered to the child's eye. If you turn to the word "Pica" in Webster's dictionary you will find a sample of the type which is as small as should be submitted to the eyes of young children. The letter is about .07 of an inch in height. Most persons are somewhat susprised to learn what a large letter one of that size is. The other specimen of type illustrated at the same place in Webster is "Little Pica," and is about .06 of an inch in height. For the older children the "Little Pica" is not likely to prove injurious.

Tests should be made for color-blindness but the percentage of children affected is very small. Matching colors without naming them will be likely to reveal the defect. Pick out a color and ask the child to put all the others of same color with it. Do not *name* the color.

HEARING.

From nineteen to twenty-five per cent. of our school children have some difficulty in their hearing either with one or both ears. The effect of such defects on the school life is a dreaminess or inattention, a dullness or stupidity, (which may entirely disappear when the child is cured), and the execution of commands a little later than the rest of the class or at least after getting the cue by a glance at a classmate. In many children the degree of the difficulty varies at different times. In some it is accompanied by catarrhal difficulty and a tendency to sit with the mouth open. This with the dullness or stupidity of the face intensifies the impression and is perhaps a surer symptom of imperfect hearing than the effects to which I have just made reference.

There are three methods of testing the ear, first by use of a whisper, second by use of an acoumeter and third by using the ticking of a watch. An expert only should use the whisper as it is difficult to keep it at the same degree of loudness: The acoumeter is best and consists simply of an apparatus to tap on wood gently but repeatedly. Most schools are not equipped with this, however, and the watch is generally at hand and is after all fairly reliable. The method of using the whisper, watch or acoumeter is the same. Great care must be taken to see that the room is *perfectly* quiet. Any clock in the room must be stopped. All noises even though distant and faint must be stilled. If the noise is beyond our control and continuous, our test will have to be abandoned for a more favorable time and place. Having found a place where we can have absolute quiet, blindfold the subject so that he will judge from the sense of hearing alone. Cover one ear and have him present the other in a favorable position for receiving the sound. Starting at a distance at which the watch cannot be heard gradually approach asking him occasionally if he can hear. Take the watch in some way convenient to yourself and always when testing hold it in the same position. When you move, take care too that you do not ask him to listen until you have gained the new position desired. Move toward the child testing at intervals of a foot until you reach a position where he is quite certain he hears it. When this is found, move away from him again and find out how far back he can hear it. If very far behind the place where he heard it first, take it quite a little out of range and try again as before. If he hears it at or nearly at the same point as before, measure the distance from that point to the child's ear. If not, continue as before until some nearly uniform results have been gained. The time to listen may be indicated by the word "now".

If some such signal is not given, the constant listening produces fatigue and inconsistent results. The memory of the sound is sometimes a disturbing element and you may be obliged to suspend the trial for a few minutes. On more than one occasion a boy has told me, and honestly, that he heard when the watch was beyond hearing distance and in my pocket. It is frequently desirable to muffle the watch when near the limits of the child's hearing range rather than change your position, as children frequently judge that they ought to hear the watch and therefore do from the sound of your feet or dress as you move, or from your voice or their knowledge that you are near. Having tested one ear, proceed with the other in the same way. Watches vary greatly in the distances that they can be heard. I have seen some that could be heard twenty-four feet and others that could be heard scarcely three feet. To find out the degree of soundness of the child's hearing, each watch must be tried on enough persons to find out what the normal distance for that watch is. Four such trials, if the results are about the same, will be sufficient for determining the normal. Children will often be found who can hear at only half the normal distance. We are not to understand from this that the hearing is half gone but it does indicate that the child cannot hear as readily and distinctly as another, and a more favorable seat is desirable for him than for the others. Most of the cases found are those in which one ear is affected and consequently a seat favorable to his good ear is desirable. The child's parents should be urged to have the case examined by a physician, as most cases (over ninety per cent.), can be cured.

The causes of defective hearing are adenoid growths, uncleanliness, disease, (especially catarrh and scarlet fever), and pulling, boxing, or bruising the ear.

TOUCH, SMELL AND TASTE.

Child Study has not as yet made any very practical applications of tests in this field. It will therefore be dismissed with a few suggestive questions: Can the child distinguish between objects of various degrees of smoothness and roughness, between odors differing slightly in intensity or kind, or between tastes varying but a little in character? Does he feel or notice slight draughts or changes in temperature? These questions though not particularly practical tend to throw light upon the source of the child's ideas and the degree of sensitiveness peculiar to his nervous system.

MOTOR ABILITY.

If we are to call upon the children for action, as modern pedagogy is demanding, we must know more definitely what a child's natural ability is; how quickly, how accurately, how gracefully or gently, it is *right* for us to expect each child to move. There is a great difference in children and we may be inflicting the same injustice and discouragement upon a child by requiring too fine work of him in writing that we would by blaming a deaf child because he didn't understand our question. We want the best of which each child is capable and therefore not the same from all the children. From this the necessity and practicability of the test is evident.

As the first and most important test of motor ability and tendency to bodily activity, I know of nothing so instructive as a few days careful observation of the children at their play before school, after school, or at recess. There you find the *real* child and not what he would gladly seem. Take a note book and note the relative power to act of each child with reference to his (1) tendency or readiness, (2) his quickness of movement, (3) his accuracy, (4) his force or weakness, (5) his gracefulness or awkwardness, (6) his gentleness and ability to modify or adapt his expenditure of force to the amount of energy required for the movement, (7) persistence in action. In making your notes try to keep out the personal judgment based on previous experience with the children and judge solely from the data they present in their play upon this definite occasion. There is no greater evidence of tendency to self-expression through the motor activities than play. Miss Sisson in an interesting paper on the children's plays, classifies the children she observed according to the character of the games. The most significant feature of her study for motor ability was the fact that all the plays carried with them movement, but more important than that was the fact that one of her classes consisted of children who did not play very much but found their amusement "in running from one part of the yard to another, because of some passing whim —over to the faucet to get a drink, or over to the sand pile to see what the others were doing. . . . . The general quality of the plays that held and attracted the children was action."

If the child does not play it is the business of the teacher to find out what exercise it does get and what the value of it is both in building up physical health and in stimulating the child to self-expression. These observations made from play need to be supplemented by some more exact and uniform tests. Arrange the children in groups of not more than five. Have them at a given signal extend the arm or make other full arm movements as quickly as possible. Try two or three times and notice the children who always fall behind. If you choose try the quickest and the slowest of your different groups together. In the same way the other arm or a kicking movement of the leg may be tried, first with one foot and then the other. It is a game that will be entered upon with much interest. Are your results the same in all four different tests? Have the children line up ready for a race. Who starts first, who last, at the signal?

To test the finer muscles of arm and fingers have the children draw as rapidly as possible ten horizontal lines across the paper a short distance apart. If the time it takes them to count will interfere, have them start from each of the ten crosses you have already placed at the left margin of the paper. See which child does it most rapidly and which least rapidly. To test fingers have the children copy rapidly as possible a series of letters placed on the board in plain sight of all taking the test. Care should be taken that the letters are not seen until time for the test.

All of these tests, and many others similar to them, may be made a sort of game for children, one in which the children are sure to be interested and do their best, and one from which the teacher is quite likely to find some data which may show the point of difficulty in some child whose inaction, or blundering, or awkwardness, has been regarded by his teacher or his parents as pure stupidity, and punished accordingly, when, as a matter of fact, it was a case of defective motor ability, needing especial incentive to effort. The boy who does not run fast, is slow, handles himself clumsily, is the object of ridicule among his playmates, who nickname him "wooden man," or some other significant term. He does not get their encouragement in overcoming his faults by extra work and training. His stimulus in this direction must come through his teacher. If in his school life he finds himself in the same ridiculous position without hope, what wonder if he does become apathetic, still less active. and the more *shut up within himself*, i. e., less expressive of himself!

ENUNCIATION.

Although a form of motor activity, this has seemed important enough to deserve a place by itself. Not many cases of greatly arrested speech development are found in the schools, perhaps for the reason that we will not allow them there, but there are not infrequently cases of indistinct and childish enunciation. which ought to be remedied early in life, before bad habits of ear and speech are formed.

In all these cases the essential for a test is not to trust to noticing errors and correcting them as best we can in class. The child to be examined must be taken by himself and asked to pronounce after you a list of words containing almost all the common sounds and combinations of them. Where errors are found they must be noted, and then, as soon as the list is finished, a systematic attempt must be made to lead the child to the correct pronunciation. The following list is recommended, though by no means complete. Some words apparently unnecessary are added as they have shown themselves desirable.

cat	run	pig	bed	milk	hop
jump	have	chin	this	shall	awl
sing	see	walk	tax	buzz	book
me	out	call	yes	large	pure
fur	eat	whip	love	funny	kite
put	food	bar	boy	is	fall
on	new	make	lie	grass	oil
girl	sail	quick	her	warm	rope
hitch	place	pleasure	my	thank	boat
say	move	face	and	fun	

Some sounds must be heard and attempted for a number of days before they are perfected, but great help is gained if you can find another word containing the same sound, this time correctly pronounced by the child.

Sometimes the peculiar habit, stammering, which is an affection of the muscles and often an example of misapplied imitation, is found in our schools. No tests are necessary in this case. Sometimes the cure is comparatively simple. Always speaking with chest well filled, never speaking in a hurry will do much toward giving confidence, which is one essential for a cure. Practice in reading rythmical sentences slowly and deliberately helps also, as does the performance of some slight muscular action just as the difficult word is pronounced. The movement of a finger is sufficient after practice to cure some cases.

The cause as has been hinted is either imitating consciously or unconsciously some one who stammers, or it is carelessness in speaking. Nervousness and excitement tend to increase the difficulty.

NERVOUSNESS.

All of our schools have their quota of nervous children; some of them irritable, some of them excitable, all of them restless and impatient of the teacher's next move. The causes are almost too numerous to warrant an attempt to mention them. Some of the most important are insufficient food and irregular times for eating it, lack of sleep, bad air in schoolroom, difficulty with work, heredity, use of tobacco, nervousness in manner of the teacher, most forms of disease, unhigenic condition of home, school or person, adolescence, fatigue, and so fourth. The removal of the unfavorable conditions will greatly improve matters, but not infrequently a physician will have to be consulted before the real cause will appear.

My belief is that teachers usually center on certain ones as the nervous children of the class, and on certain others as absolutely free from any such defect. Those in between are not classified. To include all, and also to act as a proof of the accuracy of our observation, (*not* to supplant it) we should test the children in some uniform way. The best test that I know is the command to the children, soon after the opening, to rise and stretch out their arms and hands horizontally in the same plane as the body. Have them hold the position a moment. Notice the quivering and twitching fingers, and you have an indication as to the nervous children of your class, though there may be some few whom you have not discovered. These will not be the very nervous ones, however, but those who have energy enough to nerve themselves up to the task at hand.

FATIGUE.

The same tests described under the head of nervousness are the best ones I know with regard to fatigue, but they should be tried in this case at the close of the school or after the fatigueing exercise. I have detected a decided difference in tests made before and after a single severe mental exercise.

A great deal of time has been given to tests of fatigue by students of child study but the results have thus far given us averages for average exercises under average conditions, and are adapted rather to statistical study than the needs of the ordinary school room. Perhaps the most important result has been the proof of the economy of the short recitation period over the long, especially in lower grades. This scientific study of fatigue has produced a slight reaction against this line of investigation and has caused the remark "that both we and the children have to get tired sometimes." True as that statement may be, we know well that we should find out what children tire most easily and, if possible, the reason. It may be the first sign of some insidious disease. We know, too, that the clearness of the ideas aroused under our instruction is very dependent on the child's freshness. Enthusiasm is almost impossible for any of us when we are tired out. When a child is found in such a condition, we must recognize the fact. If we cannot remove the cause and therefore the fact, the child should be removed from school or his work lightened, until his recovery of himself is assured.

DISEASE.

Child study involves the effect on the child of bad conditions. Tuberculosis, rickets, bronchitis, catarrh and headaches are brought on and aggravated by impure air, cholera by fatigue of the muscles, spinal diseases by bad posture in sitting or in writing, indigestion and constipation by too much restraint and sedentary occupation, bad eyes by bad positions of book or paper or light, nervousness by too much pressure, too much worry and last but by no means least by nervousness in those about them in which it is possible that the teacher is at fault. Cigarette smoking is an evil that deserves attention by itself. It tends to nervousness of the physical type and to stupidity.

Child study has shown that the past record of the child for health should be inquired into by the teacher as throwing light on present or future conditions. No sick child should be encouraged to stay at school. On every account it is safer that the child be at home. Isolation of outbreaks of scarlet fever and diphtheria reduces the number of cases to one-sixth of what it would be otherwise. The number of deaths is in each proportional to the number of cases.

GROWTH.

Dr. Bayard Holmes has so excellently treated this subject that I take the liberty of quoting his results and referring my readers to his article for his arguments and his references. There is also to be found the table of normal height and normal girth of children from the ages six to twenty formed by measurement of St. Louis school children by William Townsend Porter.

1. There is a regular order of physical growth in the child. The normal curves of growth for boys and girls are quite different. No individual child conforms exactly to this curve, but each one follows its sequence closely. The order of growth is practically invariable and deviations in time are not considerable.

2. This regular order in physical development is synchronous with a co-ordinate development of the faculties and functions of the mind.

3. Normal physical growth is interrupted, defeated or dwarfed by (1) inadequate food and clothing, (2) injuries and diseases, (3) improper over-stimulating or under-stimulating environments, (4) artificial restraint and (5) untimely toil.

4. When a child fails for cause to attain its normal growth and development at any period of acceleration, then he never succeeds in making up this growth and development, no matter how favorable his subsequent environment may be, and these defects dwarf and distort all subsequent physical and mental development.

5. The interruption in the periods of growth by inadequate food, by disease, by improper environment, by artificial restraint, and by child labor may be entirely removed and it is the duty of every teacher, as the guardian of the child, to do what can be done to accomplish this end.

Dr. Holmes's conclusion is: *A life free from want, care and toil is necessary for the mental and physical development of the child;* and since the physical stature is not complete before the 19th or 20th year of life, *every child is entitled to nineteen or twenty years of growth free from toil.*

Whenever children between the ages of thirteen and fifteen have been required to put forth nervous effort, they have shown themselves on the average less able to do so than those who were younger. A slight decrease in nervous energy seems to make itself know in the eighth and ninth years. These facts are full of significance for the teacher and should not be disregarded.

Anthropologists are interested in a large number of measurements of head and body. They are not of practical help to the teacher, however, except the two mentioned above, by which bad conditions are implied if a child falls below the normal.

ADOLESCENCE.

From the ages twelve to fourteen in the life of a girl and fourteen to sixteen in that of a boy is a period which marks the end of child study and the beginning of man study. The phenomena leading to this period and from it are not infrequently accompanied by disease, restlessness, stubbornness, apparent irresponsibility. The continuous control over motor centers for a long time is difficult.

Heredity asserts itself strongly here. In some cases weakness and in others energy manifest themselves. It is the age of running away from school, of restlessness, of boyish enthusiasm. It is the time when the man with his hopes, his ambitions, begins to be felt. The teacher should study each case, adapting herself as far as possible to each, allowing free play of natural activities.

The girl should be warned against fatigue and strain at critical periods and should have the full confidence of her mother. The boy needs the same of his father and warning against villainous quack advertisements.

One of the most important results of the child study of adolescence is this conclusion, that boys and girls should have their education in separate schools during this period. It is largely due to the fact that the girl matures so much sooner than the boy.

HOME CONDITIONS.

These include food, sleep, work, and recreation, in as far as they affect the physical nature of the children.

Thin pale faces mean inadequate nourishment. It may be that the child does not get nourishing food. Perhaps it will not eat it. Possibly it has some disease interfering with assimilation

Sleep may be insufficient. Children should have ten or eleven hours and older persons eight or nine each night. Statistics go to show that from five to eight per cent. more cases of illness are found among children having less than this amount. A very little effort will enable the teacher to ascertain the essential points regarding the child's sleep and food.

Some children are required or choose to do several hours of labor each day, sometimes recreative, sometimes not. The same amount of school work cannot be expected of a child who practices on the piano two hours a day that could be of a child not fatigued by other forms of work. Insistence on continued work is likely to result in nervousness and breakdown. The boy who should take his recreation in the open air may tend to spend it in indoor games or reading. His exercise may be otherwise objectionable. A word or suggestion by the teacher to the children, or parent is usually sufficient to improve these conditions, and she should therefore seek to gain a knowledge of the difficulty. The parents are usually as interested in their children as we are.

SCHOOL CONDITIONS.

The school should be built on ground well drained, with no swamp or standing water near.

The lighting of the school house has already been discussed.

The heating should be by hot air with forced ventilation. Where a child has to sit near a stove the thermometer may reach 85° when it is barely 60° for a boy near the door. Ward off the heat by screens. If the ventilation must come through the windows, (a dangerous measure in our climate,) place a board in such a position that it will intercept the cold air and force it upward into the middle of the room. The normal temperature is 65° to 70°.

Whenever carbonic acid gas is present in a school room to the extent of 6 parts to 10,000 of pure air, organic matter enough to poison the air is present. It produces fatigue, drowsiness and stupidity in the children. If it can be detected by its odor to one coming in from out of doors, the room is in need of ventilation.

It should be possible to lower or raise the desks. The cover should slide down to meet the child as he writes. The seats should also be adjustable, so that the feet will rest squarely on the floor. Three sizes of seats and desks should be found in every average schoolroom.

To avoid possibility of germs of disease being stirred up with dust from the floor, it should be sprinkled with a little chopped straw, previously soaked in a weak solution of chloride of lime and then swept once a day. The solution may be made by taking a pound of chloride of lime for four or five gallons of water.

Teachers should be careful to insist on correct positions and postures on the part of the children in standing, sitting and marching.

The sources of bad odors should be discovered and the causes removed.

CONCLUSION.

In describing children it is useful to classify them according to temperament, but hasty conclusions should not be made on the basis of one or two physical likenesses. Few children are typical. In some cases it is useful to know the heredity of the child, but our judgment should be based on actual observations, and not on inference from the characteristics of his parents.

It is not intended that all of these tests be tried on every child. They are rather to offer suggestion and help where the demeanor of some child baffles solution.

PART IV.

SUGGESTIONS FOR THE STUDY OF CHILDREN'S WILLS.

BY A. W. RANKIN.

The will is "The faculty of conscious, and especially of deliberate, action."—*Century Dictionary*.

"In a broader sense, it [the education of the will] means the whole of one's training to moral and prudential conduct, and of one's learning to adapt means to ends, involving the 'association of ideas,' in all its varieties and complications, together with the power of inhibiting impulses irrelevant to the ends desired, and of initiating movements contributary thereto."
—*James*.

1. Set the children a task involving a series of acts at regular intervals; such as observations of the weather or of the growth of plants or animals, the reading of a good book in regular installments. Note the difference in ability of children to carry out such directions and find the causes of this difference in the nature of the children or in that of their surroundings.

2. Study leaders in children's games and analyze the causes of the power of leadership.

3. Make a special study of the influence of regularly required home "chores" upon the ability of children to stick to a definite line of action.

4. Notice how long pupils can keep their attention upon lessons without having it attracted by anything else going on in the room.

5. How quickly can they concentrate upon a task after finishing another or after an intermission?

6. Notice differences in the power to control muscles as one evidence of will power.

7. Notice what power the different pupils have to change habits when they try.

8. Notice how long the effects of correction by the teacher or good resolutions by the pupil last in different cases and thus find out when to give a fresh stimulus.

9. Notice how far the child seems to have permanent ideals as to what he shall do or be, and how far he is influenced by recent suggestions from others or by momentary impulses of his own.

10. Are his motives largely selfish, or does he show considerable desire to give others pleasure.

11. Is the child influenced most by prospects of immediate pleasure or pain, or by the thought of more remote advantages to come after some weeks or years.

12. Notice whether he shows persistence in some activities of work or play and not in others, and, if he does, study to find how you may link other things with these chief lines of interest.

13. Notice whether failure to perform a task well is due (*a*) to imperfect knowledge of what is to be done, (*b*) lack of knowledge of the means by which it may be done, (*c*) want of appreciation of the desirability or necessity of doing it, (*d*) want of confidence in his own ability to do it, then apply the proper corrective. (Teachers often assign lessons so indefinitely that pupils do not know just what to do or how to do it.)

15. When children have occasion to make a choice or decision notice how quickly they make it and how persistently the different ones adhere to it.

PART V.

MORAL DEVELOPMENT OF CHILDREN.

Miss Blaisdell who was to have prepared the suggestions on this phase of child nature did not get them ready in time to print. It is hoped however that the association will have the benefit of her suggestions in the near future.

In the meantime interesting and valuable information can be gotten in regard to children's moral ideas by having pupils answer the following questions:

1. Name five things that are right or good and five that are wrong or bad and state why they are good or bad.

2. A child six years old threw a pretty china cup on the floor and broke it. Its mother had never said that it must not break things. What should she do or say to the child.

3. If you were a teacher and a pupil did something which you had told your pupils they must not do, what would you do about it?

4. If you had not told your pupils what they must not do and one of them did something he knew would bother other pupils so they could not study what would you do about it?

5. A number of people went to an island to live and at first they did not have any laws. One of them stole from the others. Should he have been punished and if so how? They then made a law that no one should steal. Another man soon afterwards stole something. Should he have been punished and if so, how?

CHILD STUDY LITERATURE.

BOOKS.

1. Baldwin—Mental Development in the Child and the Race. Macmillan Co., New York City. Price $2.60.
2. Barnes—Studies in Education. (Ten pamphlets, paged, ready to bind in a single volume.) Leland Stanford University. Price $1.50 (can be supplied to members of the Association *this* year for 75 cents).
2. Comparye—Intellectual and Moral Development of Children. D. Appleton & Co., N. Y. Price $1.50.
4. Donaldson—Growth of the Brain. Scribners & Co., New York. Price $1.25.
5. Dubois—Beckonings of Little Hands. J. Wattles & Co., Philadelphia. Price $1.00.
6. Harrison—A Study of Child Nature. Published by Chicago Kindergarten College. Price $1.00.
7. Haskell—Child Observation. D. C. Heath & Co. Price $1.50.
8. Hall—Topical Syllabi. By the author, Worcester, Mass. Most of them republished in Pedagogical Seminary and many of them in Transactions of Illinois Child Study Society.
9. Hall—Contents of Children's Minds on Entering School. E. L. Kellogg & Co., New York City. Price 25 cents.
9½. Jackman, Mrs.—How to Organize Round Tables. Werner & Co. Price 25 cents.
10. Preyer—The Mind of the Child. D. Appleton & Co., New York. Two volumes, price per volume $1.50.
Preyer—Mental Development of the Child. D. Appleton & Co., New York. Two volumes, price per volume $1.00. (A condesation of the above).
11. Perez—First Three Years of Childhood. C. W. Bardeen, Syracuse, N. Y. Price $1.00.
12. Shinn—Development of a Child. Published by University of California. Price 50 cents.
13. Sully—Studies in Childhood. D. Appleton & Co., New York. Price $2.50.
14. Warner—Mental Faculty. Macmillan Co., N. Y. Price 90 cents.
14½. Tracy—Psychology of Childhood. D. C. Heath & Co. Price 90 cents.
15. Warner—Children and How to Study Them. Kegan Paul & Co., London. Price 60 cents.
16. Wiltse—Place of the Story in Early Education. Ginn & Co. Price 60 cents.
18. Wiggin—Children's Rights. Houghton, Mifflin & Co., Cambridge, Mass. Price $1.00.

PERIODICALS.

18. Child Study Monthly, Chicago, Ill. Price $1.00. (It can be furnished to members this year for 65c.)

19. Pedagogical Seminary, Worcester, Mass. Price $4.00. (This can be furnished to members for $3.00.)

PERIODICALS REFERRED TO BELOW BUT NOT DEVOTED WHOLLY TO CHILD STUDY.

20. Educational Review.

21. Northwestern Journal of Education, Lincoln, Neb. July numbers, 1896 and 1897, devoted wholly to child study. Price 25c each.

22. Popular Science Monthly.

23. Science.

24. The Proceedings of the National Educational Association.

25. The Transactions of the Illinois Society for Child Study, C. C. Van Liew, Sec., Normal, Ill. Price of Vol. I $1.00, two numbers of Vol. II 50c.

26. Education.

27. Psychological Review.

28. American Journal of Psychology.

Those who wish to read up on special topics will find the following specific references valuable. The numbers indicate the books and journals named above.

Mental Images and Imagination—27, Vol. I., p. 496; 24, 1896, p. 779; 19, Vol. II., p. 204 and 107; 19, Vol. III., p. 97; 20, Vol. V., p. 257 and 467; 22, Vol. XVIII., p. 64; 22, Vol. XVI., p. 106; 22, Vol. XLII., p. 60.

Memory—28, Vol. V., p. 356; 28, Vol. VI., p. 247 and 433; 28, Vol. IV., p. 1; 27, Vol. I., p. 453 and 602; 23, (N. S.) Vol. II., p. 761; 20, Vol. II., p. 442; 20, Vol. IV., p. 298; 22, Vol. XXXIII., p. 597.

Language Development—23, Vol. XXIII., p. 18; 20, Vol. IX., p. 52; 20, Vol. VII., p. 467; 22, Vol. XXX., p. 712; 22, Vol. IX., p. 129; 22, Vol. XIII., p. 587; 23, Vol. XVI., p. 305; 23, Vol. XXIII., p. 107 and 175; 19, Vol. III., p. 424; 26, Sept. and Oct. 1888; 19, Vol. I., p. 257; 28, Vol. VI., p. 107; 10; 14½ Chap. V.

Sight—20, Vol. III., p. 348; 18, Vol., III., No. 1, p. 26; 18, Vol. I., No. 6, p. 167; 18, Vol. II., No. 10, p. 627; 26, Vol. XVII., No. 7, p. 400.

Hearing—19, Vol. II., No. 3, p. 397; 18, Vol. I., No. 4, p. 97; 18, Vol. I., No. 6, p. 171; 18, Vol. I., No. 8, p. 259.

Motor Ability—19, Vol. III., p. 9; 18, Vol. III., No. 1, p. 14; 24, Vol. II., No. 1, p. 8; 19, Vol. III., No. 1, p. 97; Studies from Yale Univ. Vol. 2, p. 114; 28, Vol. V., p. 125.

Enunciation—18, Vol. II., No. 11, p. 665.

Nervousness—18, Vol. I., No. 5, p. 140; 24, Vol. II., No. 1, p. 33.

Fatigue—19, Vol. II., No. 1, p. 102; 24, Vol. II., No. 2, p. 109; 19, Vol. III., No. 2, p. 213.

Disease—24, Vol. II., No. 2, p. 60; 18, Vol. III., No. 1, p. 8; 18, Vol. II., No. 8, p. 501.

Growth—22, Vol. XI., p. 28; 18, Vol. I., No. 4, p. 109; 24, Vol. II., No. 2, p. 201; 28, Vol. I., p. 209.

Adolescence—19, Vol. I., No. 2; 24, Vol. I., No. 2, p. 70; 19, Vol. V., No. 1, p. 61; 19, Vol. II., No. 2; 28, Vol. VI., No. 1; Practical Child Study, p. 89-96; 18, Vol. I., No. 1.

Home Conditions—24, Vol. II., No. 1, p. 8; 26, Vol. XVII., p. 404.

School Conditions—24, Vol. I., No. 3, p. 53; 19, Vol. II., No. 2; 18, Vol. II., No. 8, p. 488.

Those who know nothing about psychology will find such books as the following valuable: Ladd's Primer of Psychology, Scribners; Krohn's Practical Psychology, Werner Co.; Gordy's Lessons in Psychology, Ohio Pub. Co., Athens, O.; Halleck's Psychology and Psychic Culture, American Book Co.; Kirkpatrick's Inductive Psychology, Kellogg & Co. Those wishing to do more advanced work should study such works as, James' Psychology and Baldwin's Psychology, both published by Holt & Co. Titchner's Outlines of Psychology, Macmillan; Ladd's Psychology Descriptive and Explanatory, Scribners; Sully's Handbook of Psychology, Appletons; Ziehen's Physiological Psychology, Swan, Sonnenschein & Co.; Hoefding's Outlines of Psychology, Macmillan Co.; Dewey's Psychology, Harpers.

FACILITY
0

UNIVERSITY OF CALIFORNIA LIBRARY
Los Angeles

This book is DUE on the last date stamped below.

Form L9-17m-8,'55(B3339s4)444

CPSIA information can be obtained
at www.ICGtesting.com
Printed in the USA
BVHW081847191118
533535BV00016B/487/P